CRYING ON THE SUBWAY

Priya Solanki

*to Bob and Colin,
for seeing me through my many
messy moments*

yes I'm that girl crying on the subway

yes I'm that girl who melted into a pool of sweat while waiting for the subway (while also crying)

thank you for telling me you like my coat because it marginally helped and while that may sound like nothing every little bit helps when you're this depressed - to the girl on the subway

making out in the bar while drunk doesn't count

making out in the back of the cab doesn't count

sleeping with me three days after you got dumped by your girlfriend of five years doesn't count

it didn't count

i didn't count

i didn't count it

your voice made me sick

i am good enough

someone please hire me

i'm funny i swear

hahahaha i'm not depressed, you are

but yes i'm depressed

when did a list of accomplishments become so annoying

why is mine so short?

either i'm not annoying or not successful

is this tweet on brand?

fuck it I'm tweeting it

why does social media dictate my brand

"performance of self" my ass

fuck you for telling me to come out

is this enough emotion for you

fuck love

the guy I slept with on Wednesday is engaged. It's Saturday.

did you only text me because you wanted to fuck me

did I only sleep with you because she broke up with me

is 9 am too early to be crying on the subway?

is 5 am too late?

the C train at 5 am is my only solace

if you haven't cried on the subway you're not really a New Yorker

if you haven't cried in the back of a cab you're not really an New Yorker

if you haven't screamed the lyrics to all-star at a stranger's party you're not really a New Yorker

if you like New York you're not really a New Yorker

if you haven't seen Alec Baldwin then you're a blessed New Yorker

one time i was crying in the back of an Uber so my driver spent the entire time talking about lizards and Jewish people to cheer me up. It worked.

is it racism if he doesn't wanna fuck me

sext: how are you doing?

someone shat in the empty cart I promise

please don't be pee please don't be pee please don't be pee

can I have emojis in my book?

ironically of course

eggplant emoji + crying emoji = water droplet emoji

did you get my text

is this how u sext

wait don't get off on this stop, how else will i continue to imagine our future together

well in the fake future i made for us you were perfect so why don't you live up to that?

did you realize i was in love with you

did you care

am i still a new yorker after scraping ninety percent of the cream cheese off my bagel?

when i was in third grade my teacher asked us where we saw ourselves in ten years, and i said that I would find the cure for cancer.

Now if you asked me where i saw myself in ten years i would say a quick prayer hoping im slightly happy.

is coffee just a social lubricant or do u actually like it

what's hot and bitter? Me and coffee

but no one cared when i tweeted covfefe years ago ????

moving away, running away, same difference

Buzzfeed quiz: which rupaul's drag race queen are you?

do you think harry styles will ever love me as much as i love him

do you think harry styles is aware of how much i love him

can i venmo charge someone for emotional labor

i venmo charged him $3,000 for emotional labor

where were u when u learned about emotional labor????

where were u when harry styles' solo album dropped ???????

post-grad life is eagerly picking up every phone call in hopes it's a job offer and angrily hanging up on ur mom bc it's not

where were u when u learned about gaslighting???

who was the first person who ghosted u

who was the first person u ghosted

does it count as ghosting if he died

I facetimed my best friend last night. We talked for an hour. It made me sad.

Am i sad bc i'm drunk or am i drunk bc i'm sad?

I don't want to die but you could stab me to death and I wouldn't complain.

I do want to die

I woke up at 6 am and for a second thought you were there.

It was a dream.

Or maybe a nightmare because you've been gone for a while.

Death is weird

One day you're here, the next day you're six feet under and someone is yelling at me for not getting over you.

I wish i was invited but i didn't want to go.

Regret is seeing your blood on a blade and doing it again.

Fight me, i yell as i run the fuck away

I felt empty. I feel empty. I am empty.

"Sorry i'm depressed and not good enough and never will be and i get why you don't hang out with me it's because i'm not fun anymore and she's better than me and i just lay around and i get that this is why everyone abandons me and i get that you eventually will" -- greeting card idea

One time we sat in my car and you drove, and we talked all night and held hands and everything was okay but never will be again.

It's raining and I'm tired and one day I'll lay down and won't ever get back up.

One time we were drunk and you seemed so happy and suddenly I felt sad

I could never and will never make you as happy as someone else could.

You minded your own business and lost your mind just like me.

You texted me last night telling me not to kill myself

I ran into you today.

You asked me how I am, I said good, and you believed it.

I lied to make things better, but I only made things worse.

I lied and said that I was busy just so that our schedules would perfectly line up. You messed up and I wasted three hours.

I felt fat in every dress. It wasn't the dresses.

You looked happy in your instagram. It made me cry.

I imagine the perfect world, one with you in it but from a distance. And somehow in the end we fall in love. Regardless of how little I want to love you.

You were a replacement who broke my heart more than he ever could have by leaving.

I told you I was sad. You told me to try harder.

I told you I was going to end it. You told me nothing.

Why do my attempts feel like not enough or too much?

I will never be the right amount.

I'm laying in my bed wishing I was home, knowing that I never really had one.

You ask me why I wanted to die. I had been yelling it at you for years.

I would take all the pain to make you happy, but you wouldn't do the same.

You told me I deserved to be happy more than anyone else you knew. I sobbed because I can never believe that.

You told me you were disappointed. I told you I'd heard it before and would never be anything more.

The screams behind closed doors can always be heard.

We weren't running from you, we were running from our lives.

I'm not happy when i'm with you because I feel the burden i am.

I left crying and you didn't stop me.

I normalized my sadness so you did the same, and suddenly my feelings felt like they never mattered.

I checked my horoscope religiously in hopes it would tell me when I'd finally feel happy. Or feel anything.

Gemini in the streets, crying in the sheets

"Wanna hang out?" … "never mind i'm sure you don't"

When did feeling empty become the baseline?

why is anything else not the norm?

when did you stop being home?

where was home ever supposed to be?

why did even the idea make me jealous?

I so desperately drank to forget, only to wake up and remember

why was I only the problem and never a solution?

why did answers become so difficult to find in a world with more and more questions?

did you ever fall in love with me? why not?

do i owe you the truth?

do I seem different?

Just remember, I am my own self destructive behavior.

when did it become so easy to feel so alone with you?

you read my book and realized how fucked I really am (because of you).

I waited for your text and realized that in some way I always would be

I could have built a life in the hours i wasted waiting on you to remember me

My sadness wasn't pretty so you decided not to look

I wanted everyone to be as destructive as me

at 3 am you told me i shouldn't love him

i cried myself to sleep (again)

did you plan around me for all the wrong reasons?

i never planned on making it this far

did i ever love you?

why do i treat you like shit

why do i let you treat me like shit

you aren't the same person

i've changed, but that isn't inherently a good thing

i lost sleep over you

maybe it's because i didn't matter

god save the memes

I get drunk and think of everyone I've wronged and
everyone who has wronged me.

It's funny because the list is the same.

But who showed their cards first?

Mom, can you come pick me up? She called me ugly.

Mom, can you come pick me up? They called me fat.

Mom, can you come pick me up? I wanna die.

"Ma'am, we need you to come in, we are very worried about her mental health."

"She's fine"

"I'm fine"

Why did your sadness make me feel not good enough?

Was I good enough?

maybe you weren't good enough.

why did you die

why didn't i die

I slept with him to feel something (and because he was way out of my league)

we weren't even playing the same game.

you and me, me and him

how much money does your hometown owe u for emotional labor

do jobs who reject you owe you compensation for emotional labor

crying in the office bathroom

do you think he knows the subtweet is about him

do i declare bankruptcy at customs?

if it takes over 45 min on the train, it's a long distance relationship

i tweeted about emotional labor over four times today so you know i'm doing well

the wave of depression that hits you is scarily tangible when you have a second of happiness

i can feel the weight of my depression

who needs happiness when u have washer/dryer in unit

(i do)

i feel sad

can you tell

do u care

can you tell the guy who stood me up that all of brooklyn hates him

competition: how many guys from brooklyn have ghosted u

can i put professionally ghosted on my resume

i went vegan to lose weight for u

i miss mozzarella

it is the jeans not me, right?

wrong

i can't watch my favorite movie any more u dick

is this what drowning feels like

did you care that i was gone when you woke up

do bartenders have this much money or am i about to die: a tale about sleeping around

do u think it's a sign that i ran into you

am i even the protagonist of my life

is dying the ultimate form of ghosting

I started crying because you didn't agree with my opinion

why did yours matter so much to me

crying on my birthday

was I supposed to feel this sad?

22 isn't even old

made it further than I thought

bank notice: -$20.48 in your account

when did you realize New York changed you

when did you realize it wasn't for the better

I'm crying for six separate reasons
1.) You're dead
2.) I love you
3.) You don't love me
4.) I feel empty
5.) Depression
6.) Unclear

you shouldn't have let me fall for you

It's my birthday, I can have a panic attack if I want to

it's my birthday and I'm sitting in the MOMA crying in front of a piece of art while talking on the phone with my dead best friend's dad

the problem is that no one can ever talk on his behalf

would he be proud of me?

are you?

I'm just trying to impress you

is it working?

I don't know how I got so lucky

crying on my birthday (happy)

I thought it was real and I thought you were gone

I woke up sobbing.

If I work for match.com will I find love?

everything i say is a think piece

I got drunk and complained about you for two hours

should i just start expecting less

when will you decide to remember me

when will you decide my feelings matter

he sent me a check for $1,500 and hasn't even met me

sext: why did you ghost me

but isn't it always a threesome? you, me, and my depression

note to self: no one will ever care about you as much as you care about them

all my friends are hanging out without me

glad you didn't bother to remember

I hate u I hate u I hate u I hate u I hate u

I hate that I love u

if I ghost you what happens next

sext: thanks for forgetting about me

don't get invested

they never do.

I am my only solace

I like being alone - says the girl who is too depressed and anxious to have real friendships

pause

maybe I'll leave without telling anyone

google search: jobs far away… in media

google search: how do I make the sadness go away?

sext: don't worry, I'm never coming back.

"I hope you're doing well"

I hope you're fucking miserable without me.

I decided to leave

I told you I was leaving

I bought a last minute flight on my dad's credit card.

I hope he doesn't kill me.

crying at work

I know you saw me but kept walking

no return flight

no motivation to return

holy fuck I wanna die.

"Are you sure you want to cancel your flight?"

crying on the subway

I mattered momentarily

only when you thought I may never come back.

am I not worth being on time for?

I could have built a life in the hours I spent waiting for you to show up to your own apartment.

google: how to die as fast as possible

results: move to New York

airports at 4 am are an alternate universe

how long will it take for you to notice

I mailed you a letter

melodrama

I kept apologizing

did I even need to

I was upset with you but I apologized

will I always blame myself

I surprised my parents by being home

there is no greater pressure to succeed than when you give up

two weeks is too long

two days is too long

will this ever get published

what if you never fall in love with me

what if you do

maybe that's not what i want

I fell in love with you

but i continue to be in love with the idea of you

if i get a contracted position that means i die sooner, right

I'm just a dumb millennial who doesn't even expect basic
human decency anymore

go read ryan reynolds' twitter

I can't believe ryan reynolds is so attractive and deadpool is so ugly

i can't believe ryan reynolds only knows how to act as himself

I can't believe i've cried in every bodega in brooklyn

A job asked for my availability, and i told them i'm not emotionally available till next june

Why don't job apps ask how stable i am

on a one to ten scale how stable are you

don't lie to yourself

do bald men shave their head everyday

can you get a five o'clock shadow on your bald head

i can't believe the babadook is the new gay icon

i can't believe the babadook is featuring on Lady Gaga's new album

I can't believe Lorde is literally our lord and savior

I tried to run away from my depression

It didn't work.

will I always feel this empty

how far do I have to be to forget you

how dead do I need to be before I actually am

I got too comfortable being alone

I can't wait to be old and dead in the upper east side

Bury me in the graveyard you see on your way to laguardia

Bury me in the graveyard that is laguardia

tell me you hate me

do you think i let my life fall apart

do you think i let you emotionally abuse me for so long

Seeking: a job and roommate and better life

do you know the exact date you gave up on the world

I do

March 15th, 2013

I wonder if my parents know how depressed i am

I wonder if my parents care

I wonder if they'll ever read this

I wonder if they were ever really proud of me

I spent half my time looking up

I wonder if you're actually a star

does an afterlife exist

I think i gave up on believing a long time ago

you deserve a heaven

i'll always picture that you're there

Can you come back

even if it's just for a minute

It felt like panic was your only feeling

why did you only care when you were scared

did you even remember me otherwise

texting you made me feel infinitely better and worse at the same time

I don't think I'll ever understand how that's possible

I don't think I'll ever understand my feelings for you

Did I want a goodbye

what would I have even said

none of it would have mattered

is everything I said to you gone

forgotten.

it's 8:30 am and I'm crying over you

maybe I do deserve better

i can't call anywhere home anymore

my dad just walked up to me and said his knee is broken

Emotional abuse runs in the blood.

google search: how to tell your parents you're crying without mentioning the crippling depression

every morning for the past five months i've woken up to a job rejection, isn't life beautiful

It's not.

update : i still want to die

I didn't attempt suicide this many times for this shitty of a life

Or maybe i did

Rephrase

I didn't not attempt suicide this many times for this shitty of a life

maybe you won't know i'm back

maybe i never will be

i don't want to go back but i can't imagine not going back

how long can i run away from my problems

home is a horrible place to be when you're this depressed.

please don't lecture me, or I'll start crying

the last time I saw you I ran out sobbing

u called me at 2:30 am and I hung up sobbing.

I've been praying a lot lately, especially for a girl who knows god isn't real.

what do i do

i think it's my fault

but how can it be my fault

what am i supposed to do

fuck fuck fuck

i fucked up somewhere didn't i

how can i possibly feel like this is my fault

i think that i'll always feel guilty

i think i want to give up

i never want people to go through what i'm going through and here we are

i broke

i could never focus on myself and maybe that's what you should have realized

there is no being okay

i'm not allowed to be depressed at home

When i was nine i thought about killing myself for the first time

when i was twelve i planned the rest of my life

that plan only went two weeks into the future

a very bloody ending

you tried to kill yourself and it made me realize how alone i am

I realized i will never be more than my depression

when i was 17 i decided to end it and told you and you tried to stop me

four months later you died

"natural causes"

self care is being anywhere except new york

you randomly called me and it made me really happy

i know i can't do this

but a part of me hopes that i can

most of me hopes that i'll die

self care is watching baby driver

Kill your darlings

go watch

self care is rewatching all of avatar the last airbender AND legend of korra

i don't think i'm scared to grow old alone

but that scares me

when did you realize you wouldn't fall in love again

when did i realize you were the one for me

seventeen is young to fall in love

but i did

when do i get to fall out of love

when do i get to stop feeling sad

two days after you died i went to your church for sunday service

i cried the entire time

strangers came up to me and hugged me

in that moment i felt lucky to know your kindness

in that moment i felt so unlucky that you're dead.

going to church alone and sobbing is a weird experience

would recommend

I still don't believe in god

sorry.

please stop screaming

i kept avoiding your calls

but maybe not on purpose

i felt in my gut you weren't telling me something

that something being that maybe you hate me too

we always had an expiration

i hoped it would be further down the line

or maybe i didn't

do you think i'll ever finally get to run away

i keep looking at apartments in cities i'll never be able to afford to live in

you punched me in the boob

one time, when i was sixteen i almost fought a group of white girls

at a Neighborhood and 1975 concert

i would have won

none of my friends were going to back me up

first sign of how fake they were

I still want to die

I've been googling ways to kill myself

when will i finally do it

i've been thinking about death for thirteen years

i want to die just so you finally fucking remember me

i fucking hate you

I have applied to fifty jobs in the past two weeks

only bread smells as good as it tastes

okay the episode of avatar where they roast themselves through a shitty play is the greatest work of television art

I was sober for 21 years

which makes every story from before my 21st birthday that much more embarrassing

do you think I'll ever forget my self destructive behaviors

do you think you will

can we erase that night

scratch that

can we erase all of those nights

will I ever get over melodrama

do you think even a sliver of the future I imagine will come true

I got drunk and tried to kill myself

did I already write that

did someone else?

seeking validation

so I wrote a book that would never get published

did y'all know I wrote an actual novel

it's probably crap.

my mom wears a set of golden bangles.

she has every single day of my life

you can hear them jingle anytime she's near

the sound of her jingling bangles became the sound of my conscience

anytime I'm lost or confused or scared or lonely, I hear a faint jingle or maybe I'm just going insane

probably the latter

I'm going to wear bangles every day once I have kids

just so they have a slight warning before I come into a room

a long list of embarrassing failures aka my autobiography

I had an idea but forgot it

I wrote happy birthday on my dead best friend's Facebook wall because nothing is real

maybe we never were.

I lost you a long time ago

supercut

do you think lorde wrote liability about me

who would end up on my side

knowing your kindness isn't enough, is it

am i forgetting you

you don't have a middle name

sorry, permanently out of commission

what's it like to be remembered

i think you always will be

by me at least

someone is probably watching shrek right now

my dictionary recognized shrek as a real word !!!!

I used to do social media for RuPaul's Drag Race

i stopped watching because i was too depressed

I stopped doing a lot of things because i was too depressed

Little known fact: s-town is actually about new york city

i just want a cute apartment, in a city that doesn't make me want to die

and maybe someone who will love me

but i've learned that all of that is too much

i've learned not to get invested because i never get anything i really want

what a sad way to exist

but unfortunately the only way i know

being ugly is really tough

pretty people tell you that you're not, but you never get to believe it

instead you look in the mirror and hate what you see

no one asks you out

no one approaches you

you are seen as less kind

less valuable

and every single time you hear someone laughing behind you, you assume it's because you're ugly and everyone is laughing at you

they're not laughing at you though

Fun Fact: no one gives a shit about what you look like

to be honest we are all too worried about ourselves to give a shit about what you look like

but that doesn't stop me from being paranoid

i remember every single time someone has called me ugly

and i am so unlucky to never get to forget

i want to endlessly create but i'm too depressed

i lack the privilege to be able to stay

something many of you will never understand

leaving new york was the best and worst thing that ever happened to me

new york is where dreams go to die, pass it on

i fell in love in new york, so i guess i never will again

i launched my career in comedy when i was born a joke

literally every character in avatar/korra is metal as fuck

should i tweet that

i just did

if you're reading this go favorite my tweets

everything i write is garbage

don't ever forget that

i think i broke when it hurt to see you happy

i think i broke when i could never see myself happy

i think i broke when the longest i had ever been happy was three months

i don't even know if i was really happy, or if i convinced myself i was for the sake of not losing it

do yourself a favor, and never question when you're happy

do me a favor and remind me to drink water

do me a favor and listen to do me a favor

should i publish a playlist with this book

honestly just go to my spotify and listen to my playlists from s ummer 2017

or all of 2017

is it weird that i write as if someone besides myself will read this

if you're a publisher reading this then here's a list of reasons to publish this
1.)

Thanks.

just kidding

Please publish me just so this little girl from carrollton, texas can feel like there is a point to live isn't depression weird

i only exist from reason to reason

what happens when i run out of reasons

I turn to social media for validation only to find all my friends forgot about me

to be quite honest, i forgot about myself

but i forgot about myself when i was nine years old

once you decide to die, you never matter ever again

i filled the giant hole in my chest by trying to help people

i pride myself in being a good host and always having someone else's solutions

never my own.

solutions are a privilege

one i have yet to be granted

i'll run away someday

and then you'll have to forget me

i'll kill myself

and then maybe you never will

my grandpa is partially deaf, and my mom keeps yelling menial things at him

i told myself i'd write five thousand words by monday

It's sunday

That's why the last one thousand words probably suck

a deadline is a deadline, no matter who creates it

okay but every episode of jane the virgin season three makes me cry

go watch it

this book is just an extended recommendation list

also an extended self promotion

i will forever have every kendrick song stuck in my head

okay if i ask the universe for either love or a job what will come first

answer: death

self publishing: the ultimate fuck you

or the ultimate fucking yourself over

i wear my heart on the metaphorical sleeve that is my twitter

using "reply snap" in my snap story to make all life decisions

can twitter polls make all decisions for me

twitter poll: should i dump him

twitter poll: should i come out to my parents

twitter poll: should i self publish this shitty ass book

anything related to marching band is triggering

why do southerners just hang out in walmarts after midnight

I mean, we all did it

But why

""""""good enough""""""

do you think tom holland knows how adorable he is but also how stupid

what's the difference between applying to a job and sending your resume into the void of space?

nothing

I hope everyone has a good day

(except every job/man who has rejected me)

demons are just new york city realtors

do you think a circle of hell is trying to find a new york city apartment in your budget and radius

why are the in betweens so shitty

I think we are all always stuck between a rock and a hard place

The rock being living and the hard place being capitalism

I graduated college

time to work until i die

is grad school just hell 2.0

my mom yelled at me for being vegan

Whole Foods is an alternate reality where you'll find your very successful and hot doppelgänger

I have to mass produce random thoughts

honestly stop telling me rejection is learning

I've learned my lesson god !!!!

the lesson being I'm a fucking failure

it'll work out is the most annoying phrase any one can say

my little sister was born in 2008

fucking wild

if people saw who I really was I feel like no one would want to be near me

One day it's going to happen

hello science can you make it so I only emote once a year

less is preferable

I get drunk and tell people I love them because I can't tell you anymore

I don't remember the last time I told you I loved you

or appreciated you

or felt less like dying when I'm with you

I'm suspicious of anyone who misses me

the last place I saw you was an IHOP

then you died three days later

okay Dane Dehaan is amazing and underrated and we will be a beautiful couple except he is married

my type is likely to be emotionally abusive

he's cute and seems like he won't hurt me, next

she looks like she'll fuck me up for all of eternity, how can I meet her

I've had gray hairs since I was ten

stress runs in my blood

at this point I'm probably ninety percent queso

ten percent Depression

seems too low

a hundred percent Depression

everything else is just biology

I'm super indecisive and change my mind a lot and have gotten five tattoos in the last year

I hope before I die someone tattoos my name on their ass

all it takes is a following of idiots and a clickbait title

new book name

how to solve all your problems and look hot without changing anything

solution?

the fuck if I know

I'm sorry for what I tweeted when I was having a manic episode

I'm sorry for what I tweeted when I was drunk

I'm sorry for what I tweeted when I was fully capable of
reminding myself I'm not funny

hey buzzfeed write a listicle about this

or me

or cute dogs

do republicans know that guns are bad and black people are
humans

do republicans know that a clump of cells isn't a person but all
POCs are

I'm just a qpoc shakir trying to make it in the world

Tupac is definitely alive

no conspiracy, it's the fucking truth

empty coffin aka my bedroom anytime I leave

people on instagram think I have fuck my life tattooed on
my body

I know I'm stupid but I'm not an idiot

goth Toby Maguire Spider-Man is the greatest scene in all of
film history

google search: how do I turn all these fucking lemons into
tequila

vodka makes me cry

google search: am I crying vodka right now?

google search: can I inject vodka straight into my bloodstream
so I don't have to taste it

is that how drugs work?????

you had all the right advice in front of you, you just didn't take it

I've always saved my dad as daddy in my phone and horny
millennials ruined that

happy birthday captain america

why isn't captain america the president

i guess we don't need another white dude to ruin our nation

isn't it crazy how every white man has single handedly ruined
both my life and america

working on a project

send me an email to solapriy@gmail.com of anytime a man
ghosted you

email subject: fuck men

please make sure every man in your life knows that he isn't
worth your time but you are gracious enough to allow it

i came back from new york more depressed and vegan

take more pictures, it won't kill you

It'll kill you that he died, and you have a handful of photos together

it'll kill them that when you're gone they don't get to remember

go drink some red wine and sob

rules to being a good host
1.) always make food (people don't want to be demanding, but
 if you already cooked then they are going to eat it)
2.) always have alcohol
3.) fill their glass up with water/wine before it's empty (give
them a glass of water before they ask)
4.) play good music
5.) listen more than you speak
6.) have two ply toilet paper

my mom taught me to be a good host and to hate myself

is remembering a privilege

I am simultaneously lucky and unlucky to have the memory
that i do

I can't believe white people just take vacations to europe

I can't believe i'm the only one of my friends who hasn't gone
to mainland europe

I can't believe planning a family vacation isn't supposed to be
emotionally taxing

I can't believe the idea of spending extended time with your
family isn't supposed to make you want to die

how does carrollton texas have the worst dmv in all of america

are all dmv's hell

is the last circle of hell just waiting in line at the dmv for the
rest of eternity

sobbing in a lyft line is the ultimate form of emotional labor

is anyone else still hoping their beanie babies have value

is anyone else still hoping to find love in this hell hole we call new york

are baby boomers aware they ruined both america and purchasing avocados for me

I'll just build a house out of avocado toast

hey can someone buy me dinner and yell at me for an hour about being a failure, i miss my parents

the two genders are depression and anxiety

I cannot believe that my older sister invented comedy

I cannot believe my older brother invented being positive

I cannot believe that i invented hell

I cannot believe that my little sister defined the word diva

do you think every person who voted for trump is aware how much i hate them

do you think hillary knows i'd take a bullet for her

why celebrate america when you can celebrate malia obama

why celebrate when you can think about your crippling depression instead

every version of spiderman is better than any man you will ever meet, but especially homecoming

I hope every woman knows she is a goddess

where did you bury your dreams when they died

I cremated mine

million dollar idea: vegan mozzarella that actually tastes like mozzarella

any vegan who tells you they don't miss cheese is lying

any vegan that tells you vegan cheese is good is lying

does food network's chopped have bloopers?

I only root for women and POCs when I watched chopped

I love watching chopped junior because I get to see children be more successful than I will ever be

I aspire to be Alex Guarnaschelli

this rounds basket ingredients are gooey duck and all of your past regrets

I forgot my keys and my dignity at home

my dad is lowkey a terrible driver

he drifts a lot because he just doesn't pay attention to the road

I am also a terrible driver

I haven't applied to a job in two days, consequently I haven't slept in two days either

do you think hell is unemployment and moving back home

isn't it crazy how no one has ever bought me flowers in my entire life?

does god or the devil collect all the receipts?

my parents don't get why it's giving up to apply to retail jobs

I didn't just sell my soul to work at a fucking target

I guess it's time to sell my soul to grad school applications

update: still want to die

hey universe I'm ready to fucking to die

lying is too much effort

you always got caught in your lies

mostly because you would always tell me the truth and the lie at different times

I wanted to go to a Khalid concert and my sister thought I wanted to see DJ Khaled????

krishna is mad that things are pasteurized

my parents don't get how hard I worked

maybe I didn't

I got good grades and was wildly depressed

that counts for something, right

wrong

depressed kids don't get the credit we deserve

doing anything when you want to fucking die deserves a round of applause getting out of bed is a fucking nightmare

I can feel the panic attack coming on

I have no one to shave my legs for

forever exhausted

okay standing in the rain when it's warm and sunny is only fun in suburbia

but holy shit does it remind you why you're alive

but also two seconds later the crippling depression reminds you why being alive is a horrible thing

my parents already believe I won't find a job soon

if I apply to twenty jobs today will I finally be happy

if I get a job will I be happy

google search: I supposedly have to live for the next sixty years, how do I cope with this fact

hey can we bring back the plague so I can be fucking dead already

lol at my friends reading this and being wildly concerned

suicidal ideation has been my life for the last thirteen years

fun fact: my resting thought when I'm mindlessly staring is me shooting myself in the head

fucked up I know

I planned our wedding

I picked a dress, and the shoes, and a venue, and colors, and a theme

I was so wildly in love with you

And a future with you felt real

daily reminder to validate me

daily reminder to venmo me for emotional labor

I wonder if i'll ever be pretty enough or rich enough to be happy

if you're reading this, tweet me your favorite song at the moment

does anyone i know play the saxophone

text me if you do

I really don't know what i'd do with this information, but i would love to know

hey you should drink a glass of water, and maybe eat a snack

sometimes it gets better and sometimes it's been thirteen years and you're still suicidal

one time i sent a snap when i was happy and proud of my growth

a week later i told you i wanted to kill myself

growth is weird, but so is falling so far down when you know what it's like to be happy

i miss my apartment in brooklyn

I don't miss new york

I hate new york and i hate dallas and i hate depression

But most of all i hate being alive

remember when i was so consistently depressed and making no progress that even my therapist hated me

I think every white piece of clothing i own has a stain on it

can someone make a telenovela about my depressing life

making a zine about depression

send me your suggestions

every morning i ask myself how can i capitalize on my depression?

do you think you're willing to fight for me

i think i am tired of fighting for you

i spent too many months trying for what feels like nothing

If this is life i don't want it

I applied to a job for the first time in four days and immediately started sobbing

listening to LANY in the dark while applying to jobs and also crying

life is just a string of endless disappointments followed by death

happiness is a privilege the universe didn't want me to have

hey universe when is it my fucking turn

all my friends are too kind and i am so undeserving

someone asked me how I am and I started crying

one day I'll be happy or dead

bets on which one comes first

my money's on dead

just another night crying myself to sleep

if a job doesn't respond to you within two weeks they aren't going to hire you

that means the 150+ jobs I've applied to don't want to hire me

movies are cool because for two hours you get to forget about the depression

I've always believed that not everyone gets to be happy

and I've always believe that I never will be

and after a lot of living I've learned both of those things are true

how much do I have to drink to blackout my childhood

just seeking someone to be miserable with

do you ever wonder if things from your childhood were actually real

I wonder how many memories from my childhood are real

do you think you convinced yourself of memories you've had

a lot changes once you break

a lot changes when it physically hurts to keep going

do you think he knows I hate him

do you think she knows I hate her

how many of you are wondering if you are the you I'm talking about ???

how many times do I have to mentally tell someone to fuck off before it happens

how many times do I have to mentally tell someone to fall in love with me for it to happen

why isn't Hassan minhaj in love with me yet ????

empty

I'm too depressed to get out of bed

I write more on the subway than anywhere else

the subway is where dreams go to die and this book gets even more depressing somehow

I always think of things to write before I fall asleep but am too lazy to write them down

where do all of our lost thoughts go

getting ghosted by a job hurts more than getting ghosted by a boy

someone postmates me a vegan donut thanks

I got lost in a sea of job apps and depression

I don't know if i should laugh or cry

I'm just trying to forget

I should venmo everyone i know for emotional labor

sorry you know me

sorry i came into your life, showed you who i really was, and inevitably disappointed you until you gave up on me

yes that tweet is about you

honestly assuming that everyone will abandon me at some point

you did six months ago, but are trying really hard to convince yourself you didn't

alone and lonely are different

I am unlucky to experience both at the same time

I can't believe my future husband is so adorable and also not going to end up with me

I can't believe that anyone still believes in soulmates

when i was seventeen you asked me if i believed in soulmates

you did

I didn't

maybe that was the first sign

I don't know why i don't want you to be happy

someone told me they wanted me to be happy and also were upset that i wasn't

life is cool because other people stress about how constantly unhappy you are life is not cool because i'm constantly unhappy

life is also not cool because no one else should stress about my unhappiness except me

I think anyone reading this is probably stressed about my unhappiness

every kind text i ever receive makes me cry because i don't deserve it

hey y'all just wanted to announce that i'm officially giving up on getting invested

I lost you the moment were more comfortable telling someone else something over me

you lost me along time ago, and i just wouldn't let myself admit it

if you tell me i'm your best friend i'll probably cry

if you text me randomly saying you were thinking about me, i'll also probably cry

i cry a lot

mostly because i've been hurt a lot

and also because i have no control over my emotions thanks to my mental health

I can't believe no one has favorited my tweet yet

hey universe, what's up with me and my friends not being twitter influencers

hey universe, what's up with you being a complete asshole

I finally believe god is a man, because no woman could be
so cruel

is believing in god and believing in the power of the universe
the same thing

I love writing just because i love the sound of keyboard clicks

I love writing because i get the opportunity to create a universe
less cruel than this one

but for some reason all of my writing is very cruel

spoiler alert they're either going to die or end up as unhappy
as me

I write cruel universes because i secretly hope everyone else is
as unhappy as me

but i also know that the people in my life deserve all the
happiness in the world

and i'm still trying to understand how i so deeply want these
two things at the same time

there are no more original thoughts left, are there

I can't wait to see another reboot of a movie because original
thoughts are dead

I can't wait to write just another teen novel about love and
mental health

but really about heartbreak and depression

because those are the only two things i know

do you think it's healthy for me to be telling all of this to an
audience of potential strangers

do you think it's healthy that i can't go to therapy because i have trouble opening up but you are currently reading my diary

is this really a diary if you are reading it

therapy requires trust, which is something i may never have

I trust very few people

and even then i don't trust anyone with all of my secrets

if everyone i trusted got in a room together, they still wouldn't be able to crack the real me

so yes i do have a lot of issues, but i'm sure you were thinking that a long time ago

I hit my word count for the day but i'm still writing because the depression doesn't go away

I wish i could turn my depression on and off

granted i would never turn it on

or maybe i would

I self sabotage a lot

I think it's because i don't believe that i deserve to be happy

and i'm not really sure why i don't

hey can you call me and ask me about my dead best friend

I don't talk about him enough because i assume no one wants to hear about him

isn't it scary how i've locked away an entire human being into the back of my memory that no one may ever get to see

daily reminder to remind the people in your life that you love and appreciate them

every time i tell someone i love and appreciate them they assume i'm drunk or crying

honestly one of them is probably true

or both

somebody needs to stop the internet

someone needs to stop my sister

someone needs to fucking end me

hey friends stop sending me snaps of you having fun without me

I'm already very aware you don't need me without the reminder

inviting everyone I slept with over for a focus group

but we never made any moment a moment ever again

maybe we had too many

how is child acting not illegal

my sister says babies shouldn't get paid more than minimum wage

do you think I'll be a good mom

I never want to be pregnant

please call him out for breaking my heart

who needs men when stationary exists

do you think my sister heard me sobbing myself to sleep last night

you make me anxious

I think we're done

I'm too depressed to fall asleep and too depressed to ever want to wake up

I can't even imagine being happy anymore

should I invite him to coffee and tell him I'm ghosting him

what's the proper etiquette for ghosting

haven't decided if I'm going to tell you or not

do you think my doppelgänger is as miserable as me

what do you think about when you think of me

how often do you think of me

your post made me sad

you made me sad

I hate how deeply I can feel my sadness

just so you all know sadness and depression are different things

I am so fortunate to feel both at the same time

somehow I almost always can't relate

I love seeing people excited about something in their life

I'm really scared of being mad

isn't self esteem such a weird made up concept that I am so bad at

it could be my wedding day and you could tell me I'm beautiful and I still won't believe you

will still be seeking validation from you in ten years

hey can a professional psychoanalyze this book

please tell me what's wrong with me that I don't already know

sorry universe for upsetting you

I'd like to formally apologize to the universe and also every single person who I've met

why is tofu so hard to cook?

I want to feel shiny again

take me to watch a marvel movie and i'm yours

spiderman homecoming made me temporarily forget the depression

sometimes depression takes a pause

are your parents the type of parents to turn you in or help you bury the body

are you going to be the type of parent to turn them in or help bury the body

I have a weird fear of accidentally murdering someone

that's why i don't let people in the kitchen with me when i'm cooking the broccoli i cooked is too salty

do you think i'm insane

text me the answer when you read this

how do i instantly become a super famous comedian

I think i'd be pretty good at it

but i also think i'm hilarious, which i'm probably not

I think i'll be okay not seeing you again

and that says a lot in itself

I wonder if the problem is further back

I wonder if it's too far back to fix

rewind

what part of our lives will remain hidden

am i always allowed to have secrets

just tweet me your feelings

texting is dead

can i have a public group chat with everyone who has
wronged me

new social media idea: public social media pages where you
publicly add everyone you hate instead of friends

public passive aggressive posts are the new form of intimacy

hey can a venture capitalist fund this shitty idea, thanks

can the shape of the clouds determine my future already

why the fuck do people believe that the stars have anything to
 o with us

they are very lucky to have nothing to do with us

someone please tell Tom Holland i'm in love with him

okay if you don't appreciate the marvel cinematic universe then
you don't understand that Stan Lee single handedly created s
uch an intricate and dynamic universe

getting older means realizing having dreams is impractical

I'm refusing to acknowledge you

writing a tv show about finding love in New York

everyone ends up wildly alone and depressed in the end

loosely based on my life

google search: how do I make a show about depression without
making it extremely boring

what is jesus's last name?

is getting older just endlessly trying to find a new dinner spot
and giving up and settling for your normal one

why do hegemonically masculine men always drink straight
whisky

do men realize "girly" drinks have a lot more alcohol than beer
and taste better

people don't change, and i should have realized that a year ago do you imagine adam and eve as white

honestly the bible tells one hell of a story

why did white people so long ago choose the bible as the fake
story to dedicate their lives to

are you offended by that

I remember it was christmas time

and we were at your house making a gingerbread house

and i made some comment about evolution

(specifically i asked if you thought i could single handedly
evolve his pet fish to breath out of water)

and you told me you didn't believe in evolution

still confusing to me

sunrises are so pretty

we don't deserve them

do evil people realize they are evil

do toxic people realize they are toxic

I realized

did you

I remember the feeling

isn't it scary

can someone send me $10,000 so i can buy cute clothes

I just want to see pretty sunsets and to not cry all the time

why do celebrities go on dancing with the stars

are they giving up or are they just really trying to fight for their careers

why can't life be planned

rephrase

why can't things go according to my plans

you don't get the choice and that's what's hard

but life will never be as beautiful as before

I just want to be hot enough for people to think twice

the biggest lie of television is that girls are always wearing cute bras and matching underwear

I'm getting more gray hairs by the second

my eight year old sister told me i need to dye my hair

please don't add an entire concert to your snapchat or instagram story

I have yet to start using instagram story and i think it's impacting my career

the first official text about not moving back has been sent

I started crying

I would say it's going to be okay but it usually isn't

you told me you resented me and i think about that a lot

I can't wait to be properly angry at you and finally let you know it

launching myself into space next week, stay tuned

I need to own harry styles' entire wardrobe

answer the door, death is knocking

come on eileen

perks of being a wallflower always makes me cry

(the movie)

perks of being a wallflower is the only movie that is better than the book

I said that in a bookstore and random people agreed with me so it's true

I hope you know none of this is Halsey lyrics

one time bob's neighbor came over when we were drunk and kept saying "everything is blue" and then offered us cocaine

yes he was talking about the Halsey lyric

one time I told someone I'm a communications major and they told me I'd be a great voice actor because that's what they thought communications majors do

I'd love to be a voice actor

one time someone told me I look like a communications major

at what age did you realize you were becoming your parents

are you happy with that

I want to be a comedian just so I can be on celebrity chopped

If there was a vegetarian edition of chopped, I might actually do well

I spend so much time reading recipes I'll probably never make

have y'all ever tasted a gooseberry

I'm really worried that I might be allergic to a food I've never tasted and then I'll eat it and die

I still can't believe Michael died

do the bad thing

quiz: which chopped judge are you

does my lack of punctuation in this book stress you out

do the many typos

am i obligated to tell you when you are the you that i am writing about

maybe

only if you ask

should i go work at a company i hate

why are happily ever afters only for fairy tales

where is mine

okay but if unicorns never existed then why do we know exactly what they would look like

same question but for centaurs

i wonder if we would domesticate dinosaurs if we could

is jurassic park a warning or an idea

same question but about black mirror

I was crying too much so i had to stop watching

marceline

i never realized how easy it is to uproot your life

I love not knowing when i'll see you next

has publishing this piece of shit ruined literature forever

does anyone know what alt-j is actually saying

one time i was in a bidding war on facebook for alt-j tickets, and i just happen to get stuck in an elevator with the person bidding against me

is the world really that small

I lost the bidding war in case you were wondering

I hope Ezra Koenig and Matthew Gray Gubler have a podcast together someday

where they both just explain the context of all of their weird tweets

we haven't spoke since you went away

I have a headache

who will be the first one to break

it's usually me

10,000

6/10

I gotta get up early again

intertwined

come on brain

be kind

I have a lot of doubt

heavy

your turn

I have applied to so many jobs that i don't even know where to apply anymore

you think 200 applications would be enough

wrong.

oh my god

I've turned into you in the worst ways

why do parents always assume kids run late

why do parents always run late

I only run late when I'm wasting my own time

not someone else's

I just told my little sister she's only playing herself by cheating in hop scotch

my dad talking about the lyrics to his favorite song is
probably the most relatable thing he's ever done

I already have so many tattoos planned out

tattoos make me feel like art

I can't believe people my age have found the love of their lives

can someone tell my soulmate I'm sorry they don't exist

why do millennials have to be good at everything

I'm worried my resume seems fake because i have a bunch
of random things listed

but that's only because i try too hard because i'm worried
i'm not good enough

how come i didn't know cobie smulders and taran killam
are married

I can't believe the writers of how i met your mother ruined the
entire show in the final episode

I want to write a show about dating in new york that is actually
realistic

it would portray horrible parties, horrible tinder dates,
annoying boys from brooklyn, and make sure mainstream
media knows about ghosting

anyone want to help me write it

it would also show how overwhelmingly depressing living in
new york is, except for the rare moments of joy

I think i'm going back to new york

no sentence has ever scared me more than that one

can I auction off my tears for charity

the charity being paying off my student loans

I love that the student loan website legitimately says that the only way out of student loans is death

how obvious do cries of help need to be

usually mine are pretty obvious

these past two sentences are not cries for help

neither is this book

maybe

are you reading this like it's a crazy long poem

is this book a modern day epic poem

did anyone else have to read gilgamesh in high school

is that how you spell it

did that even really happen

unclear

where were you when you learned about privilege

where were you when you realized you weren't privileged

let's all bring back myspace

remember how myspace let you rank your best friends

such a weird thing, but then again everything before 2010
was weird

I want to be a professional woman who wears heels all the time
and is intimidating

people say dreams won't pay your bills but neither will my
expensive degree apparently

should i go work with a company that i know is failing just
because my friends work there

of course going to new york means ruining my entire schedule

making plans is really hard

three jobs emailed me about interviews in the same day

what have i done to please the universe

do you ever think you didn't ask to be born and then remember
the st.marks episode of broad city and tell yourself to shut up?

"you punched a bouncer, ain't you going to moon him?"

shameless episode one has horrible dialogue

weird how manslaughter and murder are different but
manslaughter maybe sounds more horrible

how do startups pay people so much

honestly I just need money

how can I be so young but in so much debt

why is tr*mp so horrible

I still don't get how the government works

tiny words that come in pairs

don't answer, it's the police

don't answer, it's my mom

"oh man I haven't said boinking in a while"

does every group have a token ho

are you the token ho

what if you're an actor and your family thinks you're a horrible actor

do you ever imagine the dads in random Disney shows actually auditioning

do Hollywood producers realize they can be racist

who is your biggest fan

are you theirs

why not

why are disney channel shows the worst part of television ever

do kids realize that the shows they watch are horrible

do we cling to thinking what we watched as children was good for nostalgia

or were the shows actually good

high school musical two has the best soundtrack of the high school musicals

I'm that bitch with a cactus tattoo

right after I got my cactus tattoo I immediately said "now everyone will know I live in Brooklyn"

at least my tattoo artist laughed

do you ever wonder when you are going to meet people who will continue to be in your life forever

I think I'll always appreciate friendship more than any romantic relationship

maybe that's why i'm bad at romantic relationships

one time i went on a date with a man with a man bun that i met in a coffee shop and i was ninety percent sure it would be my meet-cute

at the end of the date we went back to his place which was an "artist's loft" in which five other brooklyn boys lived

wasn't my meet-cute

pretty sure brooklyn boys ruined dating for everyone i know

I felt slightly happy so i didn't make my word count deadline

funny how wildly depressed is the only state i can write in

a company in portland asked me if i planned on relocating to portland

no i was just going to use snail mail to turn in all my work

how does working remotely even really work

how does anyone enjoy working from home full time unless they are a parent

you should laugh at your own jokes

but not too much

I hope before i die i play a random person in a marvel movie

I'm really scared i'm not going to ever meet Stan Lee before he dies

did i just ruin my chances by saying that

maybe

waiting for a phone interview is so nerve wracking

did i spell that right

probably not

you can tell when a company's instagram is run by someone who is not a millennial

don't judge a person by their instagram

do judge a company by their instagram

honestly do judge a book by it's cover

I don't buy books with ugly covers

do you think i'll actually self publish this in september

I'm writing five thousand words a week

my friend told me to not be that person who gets a tattoo for the sake of getting a tattoo without remembering that i have a meaningless cactus tattooed on my arm

so much of suburbia is watching chopped in an air conditioned room do you ever think about how many talented kids spend their time drawing fan-art of one direction

I can't believe there is a show about really big foods

now that's the american dream tbh

every time i think of honey i imagine a little bee throwing up which is why i don't eat it

you can tell when a company designed their logo without the help of graphic designers

I just had a terrible phone interview

still waiting for my chance to travel Europe alone

still waiting for my chance to feel slightly happy for once

I want to be on worst cooks in America just to be able to interact with these other people who can't identify onions

my mom just yelled at me for furnishing my apartment

what did luck have to do with it

going back to the physical embodiment of my depression and anxiety aka new york city!

I don't think I've ever felt more anxious or unsure in my life

is this worth my sanity

a man cut me in line at TSA because he said he was late for his flight but we are on the same flight and he's just an impatient liar

"blow all my friendships to sit in hell with you"

already done

the louvre

can you hear the silence right now

do you wish you could

I'm glad all millennials joke about death as much as I do

poor gen z is inheriting our insanity and having to do more in some way

poor gen z for this economy

poor everyone in the fucking world for this goddamn presidency

I'm so sensitive right now, I started crying while watching a disney show

could you be gentle

jungle city

can you tell I'm still listening to melodrama

I hope my life can one day be as beautiful as melodrama

I hope your life will be too

that you was anyone reading not someone specific

I always think about that scene in Jane the virgin in which alba tells Jane her life will be beautiful again but in different ways

and I think of all the beauty and joy you brought to me

and maybe I'm still waiting for that beauty

or maybe I'm just too depressed to see it.

I can't believe DJ Khaled's infant son is more successful than I will ever be

I can't believe how many ideas I have and how little motivation I have

I wrote a short story about us

you'll never read it

I can't forget you

I think I want to

if I think about my life and time too much I spiral

hyperventilating is tiring

did I already write that

if he makes you feel like a slut, drop him

if he makes you feel like less than the princess you are, drop him

I'm tired and have spent a long time waiting for death

I want to write a beautiful southern gothic novel that makes you question what exactly is your own experience with the south

I want someone to love me like I love you

it's not you.

going to do a stand up routine consisting of me just reading my most liked tweets do you endlessly support the people you are supposed to

who are you supposed to

I make people leave

read that as you wish

I'm glad your default was to attack me

I'm mad my default is to always support you

I've finally made a decision

it may not be perfect but nothing is

I haven't had alcohol in a month

Now that I'm fully detoxified I can go get trashed at a
happy hour

A leg tattoo means having to wear pants to interviews in the
middle of a disgustingly hot summer

four years later and I'm still looking for a grief counselor

I can't believe my last therapist hated me

I can't believe I was such a bitch to her

you know I want to leave

no pressure

maybe I'll be happy far far away from New York

maybe I never will be

sometimes i think i'm a sell out for ordering from starbucks, but then i consider it supporting my friend who works for starbucks

am i a real new yorker now that the homeless person who i pass on my commute remembers me and we make small talk

imaginary parties

I haven't told anyone i'm back but i have tweeted it so

I love memes that are actually just so kind

please go tweet someone why you love them

bad for us

would you be so kind and tell me why this is happening

would you be so kind and remind me why i feel this way

would you be so kind

I made a playlist of all the songs i'm referencing in this on spotify

go listen

I got a weird look on the subway for switching from listening to 4:44 to George Ezra

It's weird how many people i miss right now

it's weird that you aren't one of them

the only perk of apple music is getting to listen to 4:44

4:44 would be on my spotify playlist if possible

10,000 isn't actually 10,000

I'm not really sure anymore

the playlist is longer than it will take you read this book
probably

tweet me where you are reading this book

knowing the day of the week is a privilege

how old were you when you realized you weren't privileged

how old were you when you realized you were

please take a second to be appreciative of everything you have
and have experienced

we are so lucky and unlucky to be alive right now

make the most of that fact

caught their eyes

Beyonce singing amen in family feud is my new religion

is that offensive

sorry

all my friends think i'm insane

everyone reading this thinks i'm insane

don't worry

I know you forgot

maybe i'll be lucky to

does the mta understand that the subway actually needs to run does the mta understand that new york is known for never sleeping so why the fuck is the subway horrible after 9 pm

well it's horrible almost always, but especially after 9 pm

I'm drunk, I'll let you know when I sober up

I'm drunk and don't want to text you I love you

that says a lot

I still love you

you asked me if I'm still in love with [redacted]

I said I would be fine never seeing you again

and that says a lot more than my actual answer

the answer being no

alternative title: definitely crying in the club

I just cried about you for more than hour

I can't believe we are done

sober

there is no glueing myself back together in this city

new york city gives me ideas but stops me from writing them

I really want some mac and cheese

I'm leaving new york in four days

I'm only going to this party because the facebook event name is funny self care is leaving new york for good

I drafted the tweet i'm going to post when i officially leave

it's not quite right

if you're reading this, tweet me what you would publicly post
about leaving new york

I still wait for a job to email me

a small part of me is scared of a life outside

a bigger part of me is unhappy in new york, and isn't sure it's
new york

no place will make me happy

but new york definitely makes me unhappy

at what point will you give up on me

we are just playing chicken

how many times will i have to check if i'm happy and
answer no

I'm a thousand words behind thanks to new york

if you tell me my attitude is the problem, i will remind you
that i've been suicidal for thirteen years

do you want to reconsider

I planned too much

or maybe not enough

are you polite enough to avoid people from high school
in public

or are you rude enough to try and start awkward small talk

can you tell me why you bought this book

I hope you know i am serious about every request/question
i ask

please tweet me your responses or text me them

just let me know what question you're answering

I'll self publish a follow up book of infographics based on
what people respond

do you think love is always enough

I figured out what i want the tv show i write to be about

let me know if you want to help write it or want a character
based on you

do you ever wonder how it worked out for someone else and
if it will work out for you

someone my age just posted on instagram about their ten year
relationship anniversary with pictures of their daughter

I'm 22 as i write this

how old do you think you'll be when you settle down

officially announcing my post graduate plans: giving up

are astronauts real anymore or did technology ruin that

what do little kids dream of being now

the year i cried everyday: a memoir

who do you imagine on your front porch

I stopped imagining you

I cracked

no cocaine

I'm crying again

I haven't been truly drunk in so long

why didn't you crack

I remembered why i didn't want you

I remembered how much you hurt me

why did i cling on so much to an idea

I'm really upset with you

I'm sure you don't care

I don't think we'll make it

I can't want that anymore

I had to accept i wouldn't be happy for a long time

It's the hardest thing to accept

try telling yourself while feeling absolutely miserable that this is going to be your reality for a long time

try telling yourself that you worked so hard and it didn't pay off

try reminding yourself that hard work only pays off for certain people and you have never been one of those people

this is what i get for getting drunk

this is what happens when someone mentions you and i try to forget you

I wish i was drunk all the time so i wouldn't have to feel anything

am i an alcoholic

I really want to be happy

why don't i get to

I didn't think it would be this hard

but maybe i did

maybe i always did

the only certain thing in my life right now is being unhappy and broke

I'm so stupid

I shouldn't have sent it

i forgive and not fight

I'm not fluorescent

I have to accept it

only certain people get to be happy

maybe one day i'll be one of them

I'll probably be dead first

I can't wait to die

I'm vegan when i'm not drunk or incredibly sad

funnily enough i seem to be one or another

typically incredibly sad

I can't move forward

I'm never going to be happy am i

what's your baggage

what's mine

issues with my parents

depressed

unhappy

suicidal

self-esteem issues

do you think they noticed i'm bad at eating in front of people

in case you were wondering i still want to die

in case you were wondering i'm sobbing in public

we all like the fantasy

sometimes i really want to slap privileged people for not understanding that the steps to happiness aren't as easy as they think

typically due to lack of money

where do you hide your secrets

who would you really trust with them

you needed me

I have a rule to not like instagrams of privileged people frivolously travelling europe with their parents money

I have a rule to always like the selfie because everyone can use the validation and it doesn't hurt

I leave new york tomorrow

I've already imagined the sequel to this book

it will not be titled "still crying on the subway" in case you were wondering

but hopefully it will be published by an actual publishing house

fading

margaritas are amazing

did you know margarita means pearl in latin

did you know when i was in high school my latin class had a stuffed mascot named margarita

hey please make sure you make teachers feel appreciated

post grad life is getting drunk and complaining about unemployment

I told myself because it's my last day in new york i wouldn't take shit but i still apologized to someone who ran into me

how do you imagine you'll meet the love of your life

what's your perfect meet-cute

I remember the exact moment i met you

I am unlucky to not remember the last time i saw you as perfectly as i wish to can you hear the clock ticking

will it be hard for you to forget me

will it be hard for me to forget you

is there a greeting card for ghosting someone

when did i stop mattering to you

hey if you're out there, come back home

where do you call home

sometimes you won't call anywhere home

it'll be okay

I don't know when because i'm not

but one day it will be

can you tweet me how you're feeling right now

you only talked to me when you needed me

i realized this a long time ago but never let myself believe it

you told me it was okay to forget

I know i have to

I know this is dumb but i want to taste a ghost pepper

who do you imagine running away with

when did it stop being you

I don't have to be drunk to remember how you hurt me

I drank half a drink and complained about everyone who has wronged me

I convinced myself i was the problem

you let me convince myself i was the problem

you have to live with that fact and i don't even think you know it

everyone please watch Skam

thank god hard liquor is vegan

love at first sight doesn't exist

I fell in love with you slowly

I died a lot faster

never call yourself a slut

I love when new yorkers are mad at me because i could give less of a single fuck

it's really hard for me to be friends with white rich kids

if you make one comment that doesn't acknowledge your privilege i will never forget it

I also will only let you forget it when i stop speaking to you

you didn't buy me flowers

I don't even ever want someone to buy me flowers

but for some reason I wanted to be the girl someone wants to buy flowers for

all of this is depressing

one time when i was in middle school i went to the texas state fair to see the jonas brothers perform and i bunch of tweens kept passing out due to heat exhaustion

I told you i wouldn't tell anyone that story but here we are

I know you aren't even reading this

why did i let you hurt me

and now back to our regularly scheduled Content About Depression That Might Be a Joke (but actually isn't)

that is the title of my memoir

it's mostly just empty pages because depression means sitting around being depressed a lot

truly riveting, i know

I snapped you a picture of our future wedding venue and you didn't respond

what are you actively doing to save the bees

do you ever just think about how the bee movie is a real movie and not a collective inside joke we all share

hey don't ever talk to me about game of thrones

liking game of thrones is not a way to describe yourself when asked

you aren't special for liking harry potter or game of thrones

you also aren't special for having never read/seen harry potter or game of thrones

you're very special to me if you get my constant and stupid spongebob jokes

one time a friend and i went to an elvis depressedly concert
and got there late and as they performed we kept asking who
this band was and then left before it was over

we fucking missed elvis depressedly

when did you learn that sometimes you're going to be unhappy
and have to deal with it

when did you learn how to deal with it

i'm still learning

what will my final meal in Brooklyn, United States be?

how much will i forgive you for

I have a muji notebook that just has the names of people who
have ghosted me

(that's a joke, but not a bad idea)

do they look at you how you look at yourself or how you
actually deserve to be seen

he would do anything for her

I would never be that her

what was the first micro-aggression you faced

I can't believe my future husband wants me to pop four kids
out of my vagina

you give good advice and are infinitely kind to me when i
don't deserve it

what's the crazy thing you do when you are lost

I write letters to my dead best friend

do you think he knows

entitling this chapter of my life: booze, and tears - the tale of
post grad life

I just want to have a baby that i can dress up in cute clothes

baby boy suspenders are the greatest gift to humanity

privileged people never leave manhattan

privileged people actively choose to live in brooklyn

do you think you can make the decision

why are signatures worth anything

why do people insist on taking photos with celebrities

more specifically celebrities who they can't even name

do people realize that celebrities are human beings who don't
want to be exploited for instagram likes

do you ever wonder if you would get along with your favorite
celebrities

who do you imagine growing old with and inviting to
christmas

where is my person and when will i find them

a big part of me thought it would be you or that it was

saying it outloud ruins everything doesn't it

I remember saying it and feeling right

you don't have a grave for me to visit

I buried all of those memories as deep as i buried you
in my mind

when did you realize your parents can't answer every question

I don't think my parents ever had all the answers

don't worry, i would never expect them to

I compartmentalize my hate

I will always have a soft spot for you

I will always talk to my little sister in a different tone of voice
even when she's way older

the biggest compliment i ever received is that i'd be a great
bartender

can i plan my own funeral

do you wonder what your funeral will be like

who will give a eulogy

I will never forget yours

I miss you so much

just post the shameless selfie, you look great

are you afraid of the dark

just keep telling yourself it's going to be okay

hi my name is priya and I cried myself to sleep last night

hi my name is priya and i'm an anxious insomniac who is also
depressed which makes life unbearable

were you dependent on me

I learned to not be dependent on you

I grew thick skin you just couldn't tell because you kept
making me cry

is your twitter private or public

my twitter is public because my future employers need to know
how desperate i am for a job and also how good i am at
maintaining a brand

which one of you sons of bitches is going to get a matching
tattoo with me

what part of this makes you want to ask me if i'm okay

what part of this makes you know that the answer is
obviously no

don't worry the answer for most people is always no

really think about the moments when it's yes

glitter is always a good idea

what are your opinions on butterflies

I am afraid of butterflies because of an episode of spongebob

if you know what episode of spongebob i'm talking about
please tweet me

I just figured out why I like you so much

re: my type

you pass so many graveyards on your way to laguardia because
that's where we all will go to die

today is the day

oh honey your privilege is showing

you should really put that away because no one wants to see it

call the cops on me

love is beautiful and ugly and I simultaneously want it and
nothing to do with it

I packed my life into three suitcases

I'm leaving and I'm not coming back

no sentence has brought me such peace

run away.

how much did you believe the fever dream

how much did you want it to be true

New York subways are a beautiful place of sweat and the
smell of pee and actual pee

New York has always been a fever dream

some sweaty man's body was all over me on the subway

that's the most action I've gotten in weeks

but I definitely did not want it okay

where were you when you first heard the word meme

how long did you pronounce meme me-me

If you still do, please go ahead and stop that immediately

I caught on fire

you roasted marshmallows instead of putting me out

my favorite thing about the New York subway system is the fact I do not have to deal with it anymore

blink twice if you want it all to go away

I have a weird fear that i have constantly been pronouncing someone close to me's name wrong

how much did you really need me

do only rich people get pre-nups

what actually is a pre-nup

when do you know you're ready

how important is your friend's opinions on your significant other

my kink is love and attention

how many jobs have ghosted you

take a shot every time a job rejects you

this isn't working is it

everything is exhausting and painful

including you

including this

every time i refer to this word document as a book i almost vomit

did they remember your birthday

who did you want rory to end up with

who did you want ted to end up with

who do you want to end up with

look around, what do you see

do people at buzzfeed understand that they work for
buzzfeed

we all have names that we associate with fuck boys

the sports they are interested in says a lot about who they are

if they find baseball entertaining they just might have
no personality

if they like college football, they will always be a frat boy

this book is me making a lot of judgements about people
that are completely made up and not worth following but
might coincidentally be true

if you think they are true, let me know

do your parents have a will

who will be in charge of your digital footprint when you're
gone

I need to designate someone to tweet for me when i die

do you want to be your kids best friend

I'm very bad at this

I had the advice and i knew what i wanted but i still
couldn't do it

i'm always looking for a new therapist in case you were wondering

what would you do if you had that time back

how many times will you fall in love before it's over

okay but why would you send your kids to private school if you live in suburbia

yes i am personally @ing you

at what age do i accept defeat and become a crazy cat lady

I'm kinda allergic to cats so i may need to find a different animal

what secrets do you finally understand why you've been keeping

i'm glad that every person who lives in new york will feel relieved when they leave even if they know they'll miss it

I don't like celebrity instagrams because they don't need my likes

one time i was sobbing at a kanye concert and a drunk girl asked me if i was okay

drunk girls are so kind

are polos back

why is every item from lazy oaf worth more than my entire life

I'm just here to validate people and feel like shit

do all southwest flights get delayed

does southwest airlines understand that people have flights because they are actually trying to get places

people keep judging me for sitting on the floor of the airport
but also keep complaining about having to stand

someone not from new york said they hated it and my only
response was go hate your own fucking city

you have to earn the right of hating new york city

have you

it's a privilege to enjoy living in new york city for so many
different reasons

a lady at the airport keeps looking over at my screen and
giving me really concerned looks

i've peaked

if you're concerned for me then you aren't reading this
book right

just kidding

maybe

there is a girl standing near me that only has panty hose on
one leg somehow

can you believe that you are reading this right now

I can't

tag yourself as a song from marvin's room

which miyazaki character are you and why

sometimes i want to be rude to people on my flight to texas
but i'm not because i have to practice my southern
hospitality before i get there

ugh ugh ugh

do you believe in the multiverse theory

I do

I just hope there is a universe out there where you are alive
and well

I imagine that all of my memories continue to live different
lives than me and make different decisions

and yet i assume all of those different versions of me are
equally as unhappy

I'm losing gold

ctrl + f: a job

google search: how do i stop feeling guilty

comfortable silence

just close your eyes

I fall so easily

I was miserable

will you remember in the morning

you told me i was overreacting

you told a girl who mustered up all of her courage and spent
months beating herself up over her mental health that she's
overreacting

and i let you let me believe it

does anyone have a bumpit i can borrow

if i blocked you on social media, would you notice

I might do it anyways

god is fucking with me

what is your inner dialogue

what are you going to do tomorrow

did you remember to eat breakfast and lunch

did you know racism/sexism/homophobia make you physically ugly

what do the different people in your life bring out in you

I didn't like what they brought out

I finally said it all without crying

only took three tries

pretty sure i'm free bleeding on this four hour flight

isn't it crazy how some of the best memes are coming from our crumbling government

if you do cocaine then you're probably a rich white person with too much money and no care for the horrible impacts of drug trade

it took 18 hours for me to finally breakdown.

I'm having a panic attack because i ate my first meal of the day at 5 pm

I kept remembering that this place would never feel like home again

I can't believe i only referenced spongebob two times in this whole thing

one time i got into a car full of friends from high school i hadn't talked to in three years and they asked me how i was liking new york and i just started laughing

I liked six of his tweets, does he not realize i am flirting

I love that millennials use social media interactions as a legitimate part of figuring out whether someone has feelings for them

someone hug me I am very sensitive right now

my roommate and i went nine months without paying for electricity because con ed didn't notice us

just like you didn't!

in case you were wondering, the random punctuation is very purposeful

do dogs know how incredible they are

i wonder which species is actually smarter than human beings and i wonder when we will realize it

I know there are so many movies about apes but i'm rooting for sloths

one time we had an ice breaker at work to introduce ourselves to our new boss for the first time by saying our spirit animal and i said mine was a sloth

I'm sure he never took me seriously from that point forward

yes i am very aware that at the end of the day my online presence is worthless

remember when mini pigs were such a big deal

one time in a high school a girl came in and said her mom
was going to buy a $2000 finger monkey that would
most likely die in two weeks

I don't know if that ever happened

I also don't know if finger monkeys only live a short life
or if she was a murderer

at this point, applying to jobs is both emotional and
physical labor

tweet me what you want your wedding song to be

yes i have cried during a piano interlude at concert because
i am a mess

rain is horrible because i have hundreds of dollars of
makeup on my face

why yes i have gone to a bar and ordered an old fashioned
because of The Bell Jar

buzzfeed quiz: which disturbing sentence are you from
this book

buzzfeed quiz: which random twitter influencer are you

of course i'm not rich, my family doesn't have a banana
stand

has anyone ever successfully completed a cross word

does anyone actually like hummus

do companies understand that if i work this hard to make
a resume you shouldn't make me manually input my
work experience

I have never seen the wizard of oz

the biggest down side to texas is that there really is no
sweater season

and also the guns and republicans

what unhealthy coping mechanism do you cling on to

mine is this

I really hope tandem bicycles become a more widely used
form of transportation

if you wear flip flops in new york city, please never talk to me

I can't believe i am only 22 and have already transformed into
Lucille Bluth

everyone be nice to me, i either was just crying or am about to

does vanessa hudgens do anything besides show up at
coachella once a year

I can't believe khalid is only nineteen and more successful
than i will ever be

editing this piece of shit has included googling how to spell
alex guarnaschelli

I frequently worry that i accidentally plagiarised

I'm very stubborn and don't let men help me with my heavy
carry-ons for flights

where the skies are blue

my parents ask me if everything thing they eat is vegan even
though they aren't vegans

am i horrible person for not wanting anything to do with
my extended family

my siblings are very important people in my life and it took
me a very long time to realize that

I don't know why but whenever i really need a laugh i
watch let's play videos on youtube of people playing octodad

one time when I was fourteen some girl told me I looked
ugly in yellow and I've never worn yellow since

do all vegans stress eat oreos as much as i do

I have spent the past five months being constantly rejected
only to move home and face constant rejection from my
parents for being a failure

it never gets to be easy

we just didn't get the luck of the draw

I just want my parents to actually be proud of me

it's my mom's birthday and i'm crying because she
constantly reminds me i'm not good enough

in case you were wondering i edited out the worst parts of
this and it's still garbage

writing cover letters is a form of emotional labor

I am so glad that even my nice gestures are used against me

I am very glad that i was asked to do something by dad and
am being blamed for his idea

I am very glad that my parents are incapable of hiding their
bad attitudes and make sure that we know exactly
what is wrong

I am so glad that ever since i was in elementary school my parents made sure i knew how poor we are and are burdening my little sister with the same thing

I am so so glad my parents don't have money to fund my education but don't mind paying for marble tiles in their bathroom

how good is your poker face

would you time travel if you could

what would you change

I'm not sure i would change anything

not because i want this timeline but because i'm scared of another one

I make very questionable decisions when drunk but also when completely sober

don't apologize for calling me at 3 am

apologize for not being there when I need you

this time it's about different people

last time you didn't care and I will always remember that

once again I won't ever be that her.

start asking all the wrong questions

please don't talk to me about any of this in person

now what?